I0402585

THE CRYPTO CODE – AN ALL IN ONE HANDBOOK FOR :

-TRADING
-INVESTING
-SPOTTING EVERY TREND
-TRADE LIKE A PRO

First of all i want to thank you dear reader for purchasing my first book. I came across many possibilities and setups the last months and years in the cryptosphere and want to share my experiences. The cryptospace is a totally new, fascinating place with great individuals and many chances to achieve goals and break boundaries set for centurys. As i think this is a lifetime opportunity for wealth & freedom, everybody should take his chance serious and should try to make the best of it. That's why i'm going to share my opinios, charting techniques and market overview. I'm going to show you the most common aspects of the cryptosphere and i'm willed to convince you the best knowledge i collected in the past about financial markets, trading and the peculiarities of the new, irrational, volatile crypto market. As i want to give you a full overview i am going to show the basics in Chapter one of my book. If you are familiar with that already, it's worth a read anyways! ;-) If you play your cards right, you are able to get the royal flush!

Here are some common words you need to know in the cryptospace:

HODL – misspelled HOLD

REKT – WRECKED, DONE, GAME OVER

DYOR – Do your own research, never rely on anybody else

ATH – All time High

FUD – Fear, Uncertenty, Doubt – If some bad news come around FOMO –

Fear of Missing out (If you catch a bad trade because of greed) Whale – A

very very big holder of an asset, usually 5% of the whole supply

Satoshi – Named after Satoshi Nakamoto (Bitcoins developer). One Satoshi is the smallest sub unit of 1 Bitcoin (0,00000001 BTC)

Commit yourself to becoming an expert in all aspects of cryptocurrency (mining, fundamental & technical analysis, etc) – @secretsofcrypto

TABLE OF CONTENT

The basics

Chapter One:

What is Bitcoin, Blockchain and an Altcoin?

The Bitcoin was invented by an unknown programmer named Satoshi Nakamoto back in 2009. He was like a libertarian fighter for freedom who wanted to give power back to people. So he invented an autonomous, synonymal paymentsystem based on the blockchain technlogy. You don't need third parties like banks to send money from person a to person b. You can send funds all over the world in minutes. The blockchain is a digital, transparent ledger in which transactions are recorded chronologically and publicly. So if you send a fund from person a to person b, everbody else in the world can see it if he understands reading a block explorer. The clue is, everybody on the world who is participating in the network uses the same pool of information in the blockchain, which makes it nearly impossible for hackers to manipulate the global spread ledger, because if you i.e fake one transaction, thousands of people will see it and are comparing it with the right version of the database. This phenomen is called *dezentralization*. Decentralization is the achievement of many participants worldwide who provide nodal points in terms of computational power. These nodal points are called miners. The miners getting rewards for validating transactions trough their hashpower in the network.

As the bitcoin network got more and more public and succesful, other people realised the potential of the blockchain. They created their own payment systems, infrastructure applications and literally every other business idea on the blockchain. These projects are called altcoins. The most common altcoins everybody knows are i.e Ethereum, XRP or NEM.

As the number of altcoins is increasing rapidly, there are many new ways to invest in seemingly good, new tech startups. I want to warn you. The gems are few and far between. In comparison we can take the dotcom mania in the early 2000's. We saw endless new startups with totally great inventions. But how many of them outlived the crash of the bubble? - The fewest. Nevertheless, we see great companies today like apple, google or amazon with unimaginably returns for their early investors.

Chapter Two:

Wallets and Exchanges

Every cryptocurrency has their own wallet. You can imagine the wallet as your purse, where you store your money. The most reliable projects have a well designed, debugged user interface wallet. These are the most easiest to handle. Other, not so public projects may have an commando line wallet, which isn't that difficult at all too.

Here you can see a simple example of a Bitcoin wallet from Wikipedia. As you can see, it is really intuitive to handle.

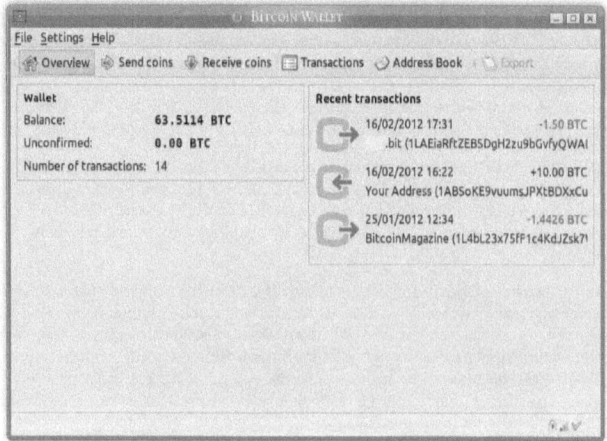

So, you want to buy Bitcoin and want to start trading?

First of all you need to find a trusted exchange. Their are many exchanges around which are selling cryptocurrencys for FIAT like Euro, USD,.. I prefered to buy and sell crypto on anycoindirect.eu. They are a fast, reliable partner for your first steps. Also Bitpanda, Kraken, and today where i'm writing this line i saw Bittrex.com also added a few USD pairs to their exchange! Wow, great times ahead!

So let's imagine you bought your first Bitcoin on an exchange of your trust. What do you do with it? Holding it, trading it, purchasing an ICO? But hey, what is an ICO?

Chapter Three:

ICOs and IPOs

As you maybe have already invested in the classical stock market, you may have heard of Initial Public Offerings – the first time when a private company raises money by offering shares to the public market. Growing companies are often using this mechanism to expand their business.

We see an equivalent circumstance in the crypto space – called Initial Coin Offerings (ICO). A new company raises money in form of cryptocurrencys (often Ethereum) and offers so-called „tokens" to participaters. In the earlyer stages of the crypto market the founders were totally happy if they found enough early investors for their project. This has changed drastically. One of my first ICOs i invested in was InsureX, the worlds first insurance platform based on the blockchain. They were happy to get the financial support to realise their projects. Nowadays, you have to make tests, learning whitepapers, join an open sale and work off their know-your-customer policy to participate. I still see a big potential in some ICOs, but i also think the market is totally overvalued at this time. Everybody who has a simple idea is able to make their own ICO, even if the idea a) doesn't need a blockchain or b) is simply not good. One of the best is Dentacoin. Dentacoin had an ICO to bring your visit at the dentist on a blockchain. A promised release was a platform, where you can rate your visit on a dentist. That's a way to good example for ICO-become-Shit. First of all, you don't need a blockchain to rate a dentist, second you can rate dentists on about 500 pages on the Internet already? As they are not even having a Whitepaper on their website, we assume that the whole project is already dead. And that's the point of ICOs. Early ICOs like Ethereum had huge profits for their investors. Not because they want to rate dentists, but because they created value to the crypto ecosystem. They established a system, were everybody can create their own decentralized application on the ether blockchain. This was a pioneering step forward, as we wouldn't see that much ICOs based on the Etheruem Blockchain today if Ether didn't developed this service.

So what to pay attention to when investing in an ICO?

You may have heard of an ICO from friends, saw an advertisement or just researched some projects on your own. (i.e on icobench.com)

The first question to ask yourself is: Do i understand, what this project is trying to develop? - If not, you are not in the right position to invest in. To invest blindly or follow masses causes more harm then gain. This is a proven fact.

So you found a project which is looking good, now you want to check out details. First of all you are reading the whitepaper and if you are familiar you will do bette reading the technical paper as well. If a project doesn't have them it's a bad sign in my eyes. Now you should ask yourself: a) Is the project giving value to the ecosystem? b) Are there smiliar projects who are solving the problem way better? c) Is a blockchain really needed for this project?

If you can answer this questions with good conscience, we should have a deeper look

in. What is the hard and the soft cap of the ICO?

The hardcap (hard capitalisation) could be discribed as the goal, the companie wants to achieve. For example: Hardcap of project XY is 25 Mio$ and they are giving away 10% of the token supply. If they reach 25Mio$, the ICO is stopped and they are start getting to work. Because of the 10% tokens giving away and the funded 25 Mio$ project XY has an estimated market capitalisation of around 250 Mio$. This circumstance leads us to the next question. Is a quarter billion dollar not a bit to much for a project, that literally delivered nothing yet? Now you should compare to projects already existing, checking their marketcaps and evaluate an attached value if the project is evolving as you think. Now imagine, their are projects with no or way to high hardcap set. We saw ICOs crowdfunding more than 100 Mio$ USD giving away about 10% of their supply. If we simply calculate the market capitalisation: 100mio$ x 10 = 1Billion $ Market capitalisation. That means a new project, never delivered anything is about to start in the top 20 of all Cryptocurrency? This is absolutely insane. These products are predestined to fail because they are just so unbelievable overvalued. After we realised this, we are looking at ICOs way smarter.

The next step should be to check the development team. Normally they are shown on the website of the project. So: We are googling their names. Do they have a linked.in profile? Where did they graduated? Are they real persons at all? After researching them for a while, we will get an good overview about their skills and their history. If everythings looks fine, the marketcap is as low as possible and the product is adding real value to the system, we found a project with potential high returns.

Formula for calculating market capitalizations:

*price per share * number of shares outstanding = market capitalzation*

If you follow these instructions, you should be able to evaluate and find projects worth it.

Now let's get to the fancier stuff!

Advanced
(Charting/Trading)

Chapter Four:

Technical Analysis

In my eyes the technical analysis of assets is one of the most reliable things to gain net worth. Some simple rules can help you to improve your trading game and to get you a profitable trader. One thing i can give you on your way is: Keeping it as simple as possible. There are many traders outthere, posting charts with about 50 trend, support, resistancelines and way to much indicators. You don't need that at all. If you combine the things i'm trying to explain with a propper risk management and a bit of logical sense, you will see that it's fully worth it. I don't want to say that more indicators are bad, i just want to convince you that you don't need to look like a Goldman-Sachs trader to make profits trading.

So, where to look at charts?

The most common website is **tradingview.com**. You can chart for free there, all you need is to set up an account. The more crypto-like art of charting is at **coinigy.com** (they use tradingview charts) but you can trade on several exchanges out of the coinigy.com interface.

First of all i want to explain you what a chart consists of. The most common and in my opinion the best way to look at a chart is the candlestick chart. But what's a candlestick? A candlestick shows the price movement of an asset in a given timeframe. For example: You can look at a Chart in 5Min, 30Min, 1h, 4h, 1D, 1Week Candlestick Charts. That means that each candlestick represents the price movement in the interval you choose.

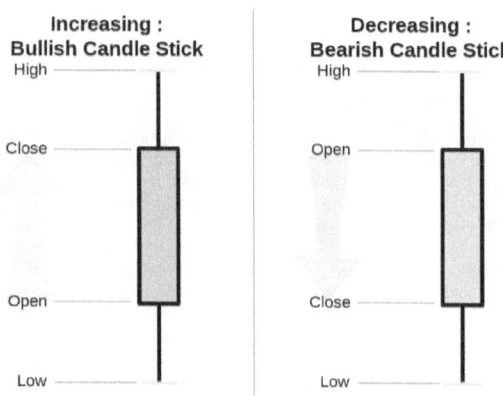

An alignment of candlesticks model a classical chart.

Here is an example for a naked chart. The chart shows the BTC/USDT trading pair on Binance.com in the 1hour per Candlestick view. USDT describes a stable crypto coin backed by the dollar. So 1 USDT should be worth 1$.

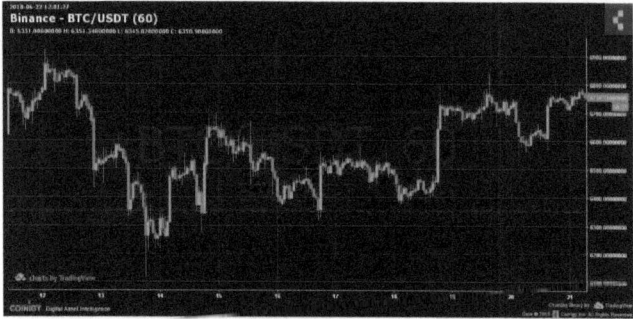

Now, how can we read a chart? What is a chart telling us? First of all you have to know that a chart has areas, which act as turning and pivot points. This areas are called *Support* and *Resistances*. A support is a zone where the price finds a bottom and starts increasing again. The resistance zone is the against player of the support. The resistance is the range where the price increase gets declined and stopped out. As you can see in the example below, the Bitcoin price is moving between the support and resistance in a *sideways movement*. We can see short and longterm support and resistance zones. Chartsignals in bigger timeframes like 4h or 1Day have more meaning than in short timeframes. This means: If you are in a major downtrend and you are seeing a upwards movement in the 1H Chart, it's more likely a correction of the downtrend than a trend reversal. Until not all bearish resistances are broken you are still in a valid downtrend.

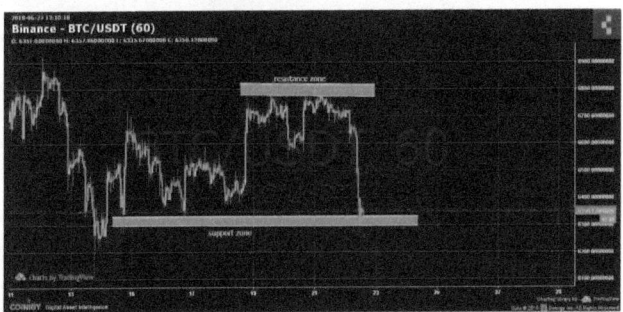

It's also relatively common, that a resistance turns to a support after it broke. A support can also become a resistance. For better understanding an example below:

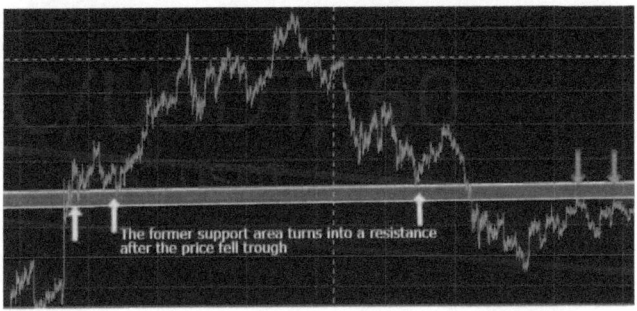

An important fact to know is that a resistance and support doesn't have to act in sideway movements. They are also coming into play in trends.

For example, we can see a *trendline support* here in the Ethereuem/USDT chart on the 1Hour timeframe. Normally a trader speaks of a trendline if you can at least collect 3 points of the chart to one line.

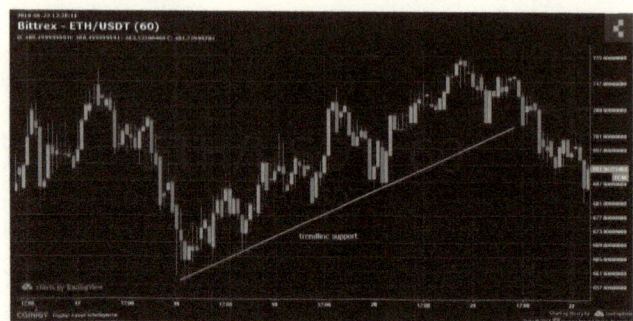

On the other hand, there are *trendline resistances*:

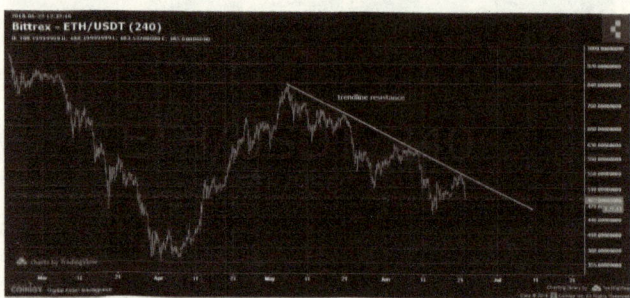

As we now know the basics of reading a chart let's dive in a bit deeper into trading. How do we know if to enter or to leave a trade? Luckily wise men invented some *indicators*, which are giving us a great view about the potential future price movement.

Indicators

Indicators are part of the technical analysis. We combine chart analysis with markettechnical analysis. Indicators can give us disclosure about the behaviour of the masses. There are many indicators outthere, but only a few a really worth to use. In the following i will show you the most common best practice indicators for succesful trading.

The RSI-Indicator First of all i want to show you the RSI-indicator. RSI stands for relative strenght index. The indicator describes if an asset is *overbought* or *oversold*. We assume that an asset which is overbought increased in price, so we are expecting people starting to *sell*. The other way, an asset that is oversold decreased in price, so we are expecting people to *buy*. The RSI is a so-called „Bottom-Indicator", this means it's shown on the bottom of a chart. First of all we are concentrating on the highs and lows as they are giving us some great insights in the markets nature. The with a circle marked points at the bottom are buy signals, the marked points at the top are sells. As you can see in the example below, the RSI Indicator is giving us reliable signals with his highs and lows. The great thing is, as the RSI is a momentum indicator it works in multiple timeframes, which means it will give reliable signals in the interval you chose! (5min, 30min, 1h, 4h, 1D,...)

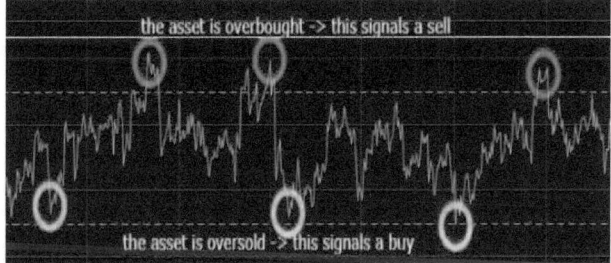

But how does the understanding of the RSI affect the reading of a chart?

In the most cases, we are seeing a decrease in price accompanied with an oversold RSI. On the other side an increasing price, which is caused of more buyers than sellers, will be recognizable of an overbought RSI.

The chart below is a sequence of the Bitcoin/USDT prive movement on the 10min timeframe. As you can see the movement of the RSI is undoubtable correlated to the change in price. We see, everytime the RSI touches the upper or the down line and peaks, the market turns around heading in the other direction. If you use the information given by the RSI you can spot some great buying and selling oppurtinities trough the day. That's the reason most traders are using the RSI. It is simple to understand but very effective   in   his   signals.

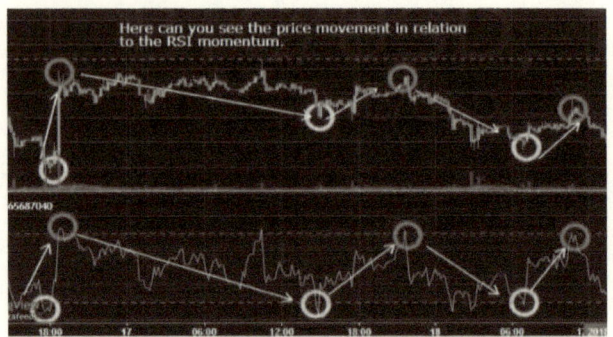

As the RSI relates the relative strength of price gains to prices losses, there are areas in the calculation which are giving information about future price movements. As the formula is calculated in a way we are getting a number between 0 – 100 as solve, there are some keypoints to know about the RSI. Values under 30 are called oversold, values under 20 are massiv oversold. On the other hand values above 70 are overbought, values over 80 are massiv overbought. Many analsyst are going a step further as the adjust the values to toe current market situation. That means: In a Bullmarket (increasing market) is the reference line for overbought assets about 40, for oversold about 80. Applied on a bearmarket (falling markets) the reference would be about 20 oversold and 60 overbought. As a technical trader isn't aware of influences he can't forsee, he is solicitous to achieve solid averages. The method to apply the RSI on current market conditions can help you to step up your average gains. But i think after you get a feeling for the market and for charts, you will use the RSI accordingly to your unique style of trading.

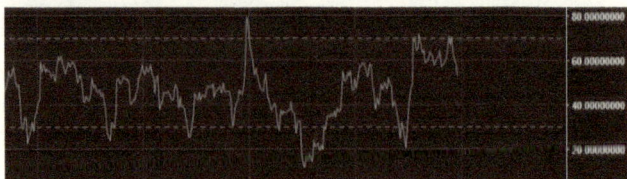

I want to show you an example for the reference values below. The numbers at the right are the points to look at:

But you should be aware of one more thing regarding to the RSI: Divergences.

Divergences

18

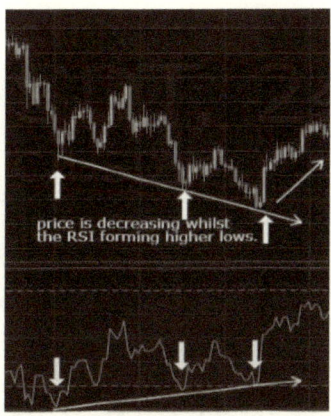

As the most trader are using the RSI for the overbought and oversold signals, many of them forget to look to imbedded divergences in the RSI. A divergence is a helpful tool to spot market reversal whilst comparing market direction and RSI direcetion. But what's a RSI divergence about? It is about to spot deviations between the marketprice and the RSI-direction. Typically we expect the RSI is following the price,the price increases, the RSI increaeses too. Divergences occur when the price is splitting from the indicator and they start heading in different directions. This situation can be observed in rising and in falling markets. A divergence is a very strong sign for the market changig his direction, a RSI divergence is a almost perfect signal for a trade. So let's have a example. In the first example you can see Bitcoin decreasing in value whilst the RSI is forming higher lows, the market turns around and starts increasing again.This is called a *bullish divergence*.

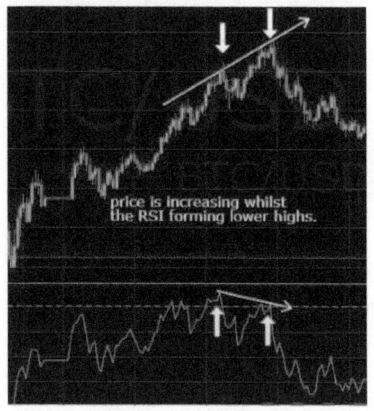

Now the exact opposit direction, a *bearish divergence*.

For the first steps, the RSI Indicator is as simple as this to use. Now let's learn more about indicators and how to apply them on the market. The next indicator we want to learn about is called the MACD.

2. The MACD-Indicator

MACD stands for Moving Average Convergence/Divergence. The MACD is also very simple to use and to understand. In Combination with the RSI you can spot oppurtinities even more effective. The MACD Indicator is an oscillating indicator. That means he swings out. The MACD is calculated by substracting the 26-Days exponential moving average from the 12-Days exponential moving average. The result of this equation is drawn as a line, the MACD-Line. On the top of the MACD-Line we are plotting a 9-Days exponential moving average, which is called the „Signal-Line". The cross-overs of these two lines are giving us Buy and Sell-Signals. So, when the MACD-Line falls below the Signal-Line it's a bearish signals which indicates a sell. Is the MACD-Line crossing the Signal-Line from the bottom up it's a bullish signal which indicates a buy. The farer the lines seperate, the stronger is the trend movement. This is called a Divergence. When the trend weakens and the lines moves towards each other again, one spaks of a convergence. Similar to the RSI, the MACD-Indicator can be used in different timeframes. So let's have a look how the MACD plays out:

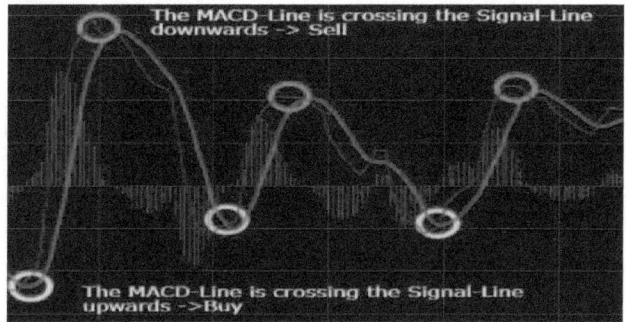

Now, as we know the RSI and the MACD, lets have a look on the Bitcoin/USDT Chart again:

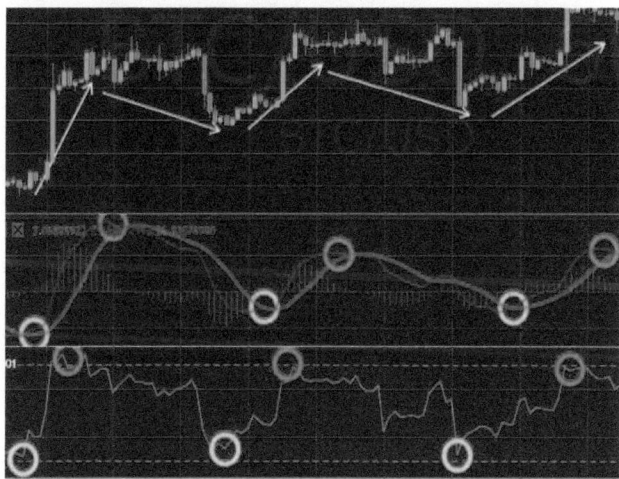

As you can see, the RSI is giving us the buy and sellsignals before the MACD. This leads as to the assumption, that the lowest price in the interval we are looking for is a bit before the MACD-Lines crosses the Signal-Line. So when we see the RSI bottomed out and is crossing up again and the MACD is about to cross in the near future, we are trying to build our position between the RSI bottom and the MACD cross. This tactic will improve our averages. On the other side regarding to sell we can see that the RSI is possible a bit to fast giving a sell signal, that's why we are waiting here for the MACD confirmation as well and sell between the RSI peak and the MACD cross.

With these two indicators on hand, you are well prepared to get a even deeper insight in the Technical Analysis. The markets tend to show us similiar *patterns* after suspicious movements again and again. Thes patterns are a sign of the investors psychology. And as many people believe in this patterns, they often tend to be a self-fullfilling prophecy. A trader speaks from *bullish continuation patterns, bearish continuation patterns and reversal patterns*.

Patterns

1. Bullish continuation patterns

    1.1 The triangle correction

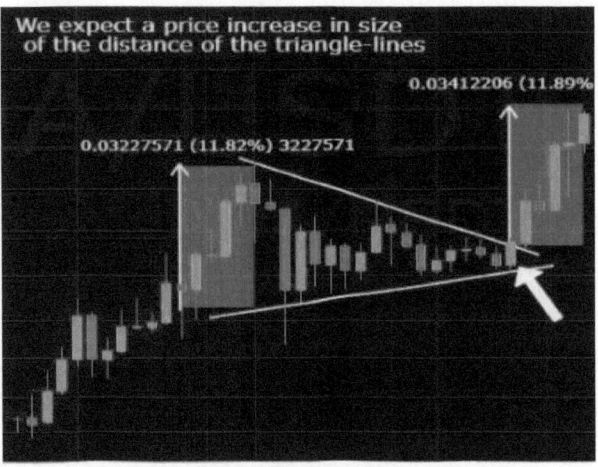

In a good market sentiment we will obiously see more bullish patterns. But what's a bullish pattern, how to spot and how to trade them? So let's pretend the asset we want to trade has risen about 12%, but now a sell-off begins and the asset starts struggling. How can we find out if this is a reversal or a continuation? We see the asset peaked, now it is forming lower highs and higher lows. What can we expect? What do we do to catch a trade like this? We are waiting for a green candle to close over our resistance line (marked with the arrow). After the candle closed we are waiting for the so-called „*retest*". This means that we are expecting the price is coming back to our broken resistance which now should act as support.

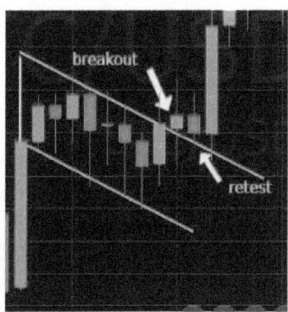

1.1 The Bullflag and the bullish pennant

1.2 A bullflag or a pennant acts just like a triangle correction. It is just another form of the market to express a correction. Because you often hardly see a difference in those two, i'm going to explain them in one. Normally we say a bullflag forms a parallel channel, a pennant acts like a falling triangle. The first picture is an example for a bullflag,

And as the wick of the candles aren't that clear, it could also possibly be a bull pennant, depending on how you draw your lines.

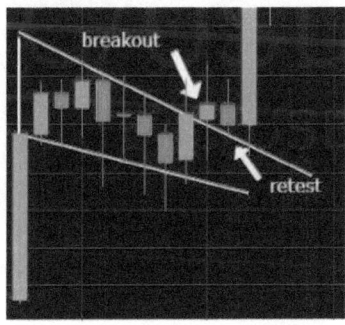

This leads us to another key wisdom – Technical Analysis is more art then science. It works because people think it works. You can give a Chart to 100 Traders, and everyone will have a different style of charting. This means only because you're individual style of drawing lines in a chart doesn't match with your opposite, his charting is not superior to yours.

1.3 The ascending triangle

The ascending triangle is formed of the asset is building higher lows and gets rejected by a particular resistance zone. After a few starts the bulls win the fight and the price moves toward the former resistance.

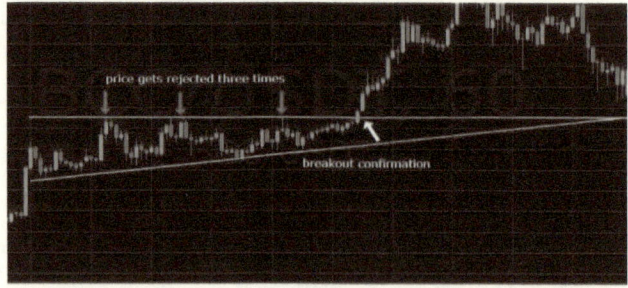

1.4 Cup and handle

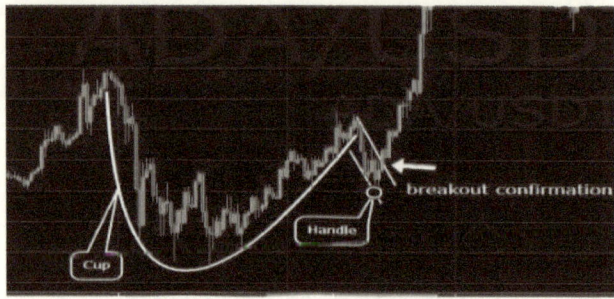

Another quite commonly pattern is the Cup & Handle pattern. We see this formation often in markets turning around, i.e after the price bottomed out and starts increasing again. The pattern is more common in bigger timeframes as 1h,4h,1D.

2. **Bearish continuation patterns**

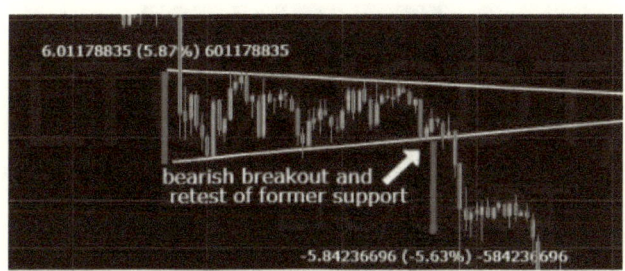

2.1 Bearish triangle

The bearish triangle is the opposite of the bullish triangle. The price in decreasing from a former high, and starts a correction forming higher lows and lower highs. With decreasing volume this pattern tends to indicate a further price decline.

2.2 The bearflag

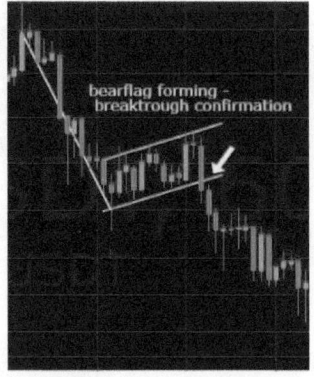

Like the previously learned bullflag and pennant their are exact opposite players in a falling market: The bearflag and the bearish pennant. The bearflag is a upwards channel correction in a declining market. The breaktrough the shortterm „Channel-support" confirms the further downtrend. The pennant works the same way.

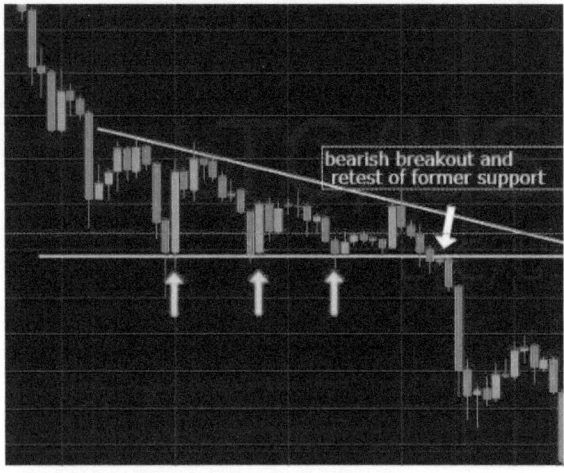

2.3 The descending triangle

The descending triangle is formed by a trendline collecting lower highs and a vertical support zone. After a few tries to break the support the bears take over and driving the price trough the former support.

1. **Reversal patterns**

Reversal patterns indicate a trend reversal, in bigger timeframes they are very useful to spot ending trends and set up takeprofits. As in conitunitation-patterns, reversal patterns are present in bullish and bearish markets. First we want to have a look on bearish reversal patterns.

3.1 The double top

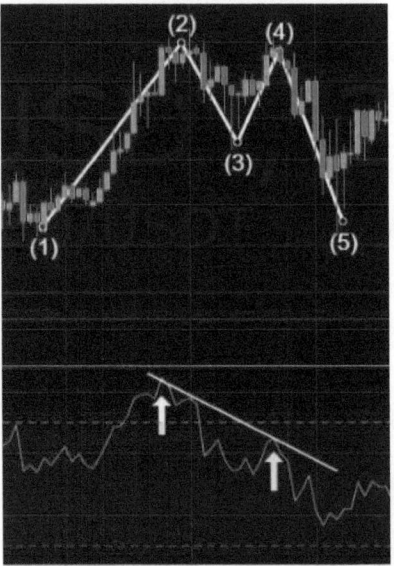

3.2 The double top pattern appears significant often and has a great influence on the
price action. It seems like the asset has peaked, the price is decreasing but then
the price is starting a new try and heads towards the former high, in many cases
the RSI is not as overbought as on the former peak. This indicates a trend
reversal. As you can see, the RSI is at (4) not as overbought as on (2). This leads
to a declining price. Realise the RSI-divergence indicating a reversal.

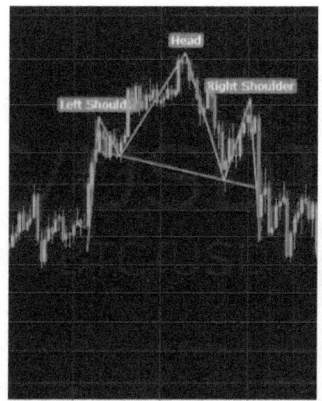

3.1 The head and shoulders

The head and shoulders – and i'm not talking of the shampoo- is one of the most common patterns in trading traditional assets. As we don't see them very often in the Cryptomarket in this form you should rather take care of the inverted head and shoulders pattern explained below. The price forms the left shoulder with a high, then drops and forms a higher high – the head. After this peak the price starts do decrease and starts a third try just about the height of the left shoulder – the right shoulder.

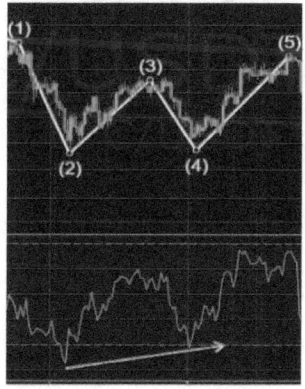

3.1 The double bottom

The double bottom pattern is quite similar to the double top. The bullish RSI divergence is to be considered here too

3.1 The inverted head and shoulders

As i think the inverted head and shoulders is one of the most common bottom indicators i got a perfect example for you. I think this is the most beautiful inverted head and shoulders ever seen in the cryptospace. The example shows Bitcoins former low in february 2018. Bitcoin nearly doubled in price in less then two weeks after showing us this pattern.

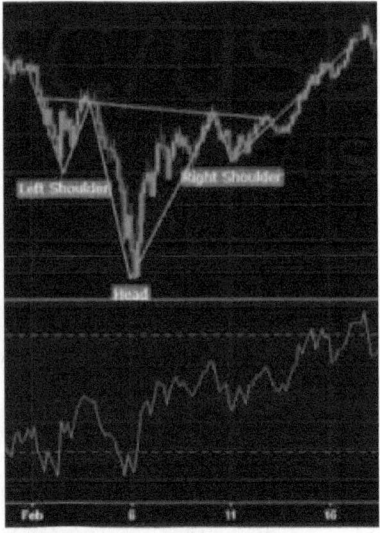

Wow! This is just so beautiful.

Now as you know the most common patterns and indicators, let's move a step further! What are markets about? Why can you earn money by trading Bitcoin or Altcoins? Because of liquidity and volatility. You can have 1 Billion Dollar in an asset, but if the asset has a daily tradingvolume of 100$ you own nothing. If there is no liquidity on the market you never gonna get rid of your holding because of the missing buyers. I remember a Scam-Ponzi-Coin named (sorry censored), they even had a price prediction in their whitepaper! (LoL) They said the price of one coin will increase to 4 Dollars within a year, their cost price was about 0.10$. And yes, the coin was tradet at 4 dollars at a particular time, but with a daily volume of 500$. You see? All the scammed old grandmas pumped

30

thousands of dollars of their savings in this coin are left behind because they never gonna have the chance to sell. That's why we are looking at the *volume* of coins now.

Volume

Volume shows us how much of an asset is traded in a given period of time.

Volume as a tool is very powerful, but many traders overlook it because it's just to simple to use. While in the longterm, technical or fundamental factors increasing assets in value, the game between buyers and sellers heading for the best price creates liquidity on the shortterm. You can see the traded volume at the bottom of your chart.

An increasing market should go hand in hand with increasing volume. If this is not the case, a price decline must be expected. Increasing price but decreasing volume show a lack of interest and is indicative for a potential *reversal*.

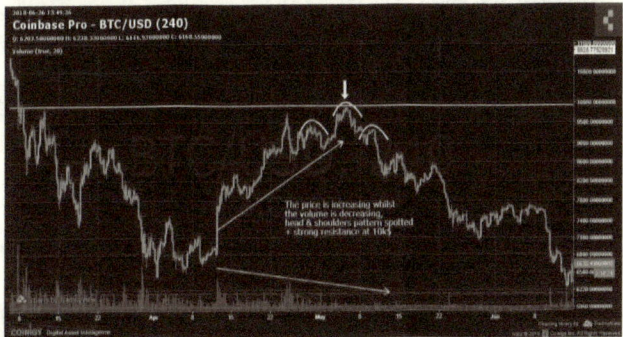

In the example below, we recognize an *increasing* price, a *decreasing* volume, a major psychological resistance at 10.000$ and a head and shoulders pattern which indicates a reversal on the Bitcoin chart. This wealth of information leads us to the expectation that the price will decline as no buying pressure comes into the market.

So we remember: Is the price increasing, but the volume is declining, it's a huge sign for a *reversal*.

The volume is also a very important sign to forecast in which direction the market will possibly head when we spot one of the patterns we learned earlier.

Volume can verify a breakout in a specific direction of a pattern.If a breakout is not covered by volume, we usually speak of a *fakeout*. It is not uncommon that i.e triangle-corrections or bullflags, even if they arise in a bullish environment, breakout downwards.

In the following you can see a fake breakout. The price is forming a bearish triangle, but then breaks out upwards. This entices many traders to get in an ill-conceived buying position because they don't want to miss out the „obvious" trend reversal. As no buying pressure sets in, the market reacts with a fast, painful against movement.

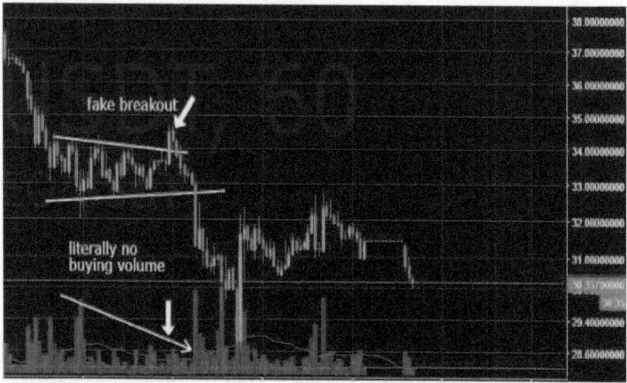

Another example for a bullish correction which normally indicates a trend continuation. In this case a massive dump appeared out of nowhere. We could suspect it was caused by irrationality of the markets or any bad news as the market recovers fast after that. We see the volume is decreasing, covered by a price decrease, but then a massiv sell volume appears which drives the price downwards.

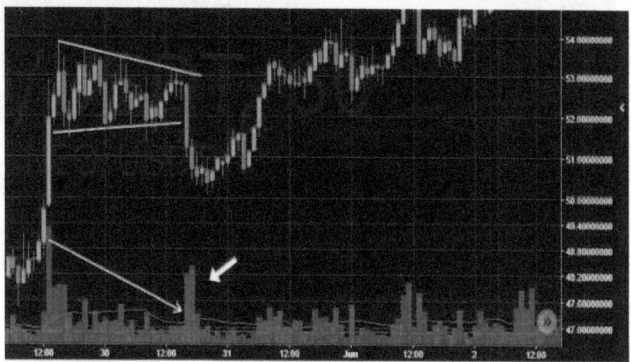

The last example shows a regular bullish breakout from an ascending triangle.

We see a triangle correction with a decreasing volume which shows us that the trend is slowing down, afterwards the buying pressure sets in again and gives us a beautiful bullish break trough the resistance.

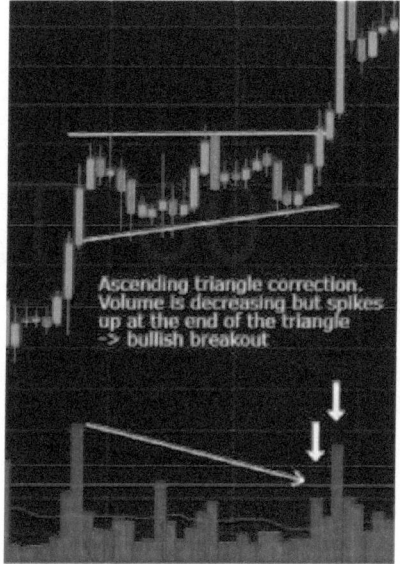

We remind some simple rules for the volume:

1. An increasing price should be covered by an increasing volume.

2. If an asset increases in price but decreases in volume, it's a sign for a potential reversal.

3. On a breakout, the volume should pick up too.

4. Breakouts often fail.

As we now are aware of many issues we have to face on the market, let's talk about the importanst substant of trading – the risk management.

Risk Management

„The essence of investment managing is the management of risks, not the management of returns.

- Benjamin Graham"

Better burn this wisdom into your skin. Really, do it! Because if you fail to prepare, you prepare to fail. It's as simple as this. Risk Management is the most essential part of succesful trading. Unfortunately, risk management is often not given the attention it deserves. You can make 90% profitable trades, but when you don't manage the loss of the other 10%, you will simply lose your money.

I want to tell you an anectode of my trading experience. When i started trading, i registered on Bitmex.com because i saw the high leverages on their tradingpairs. So i moved about 0.5BTC to my Bitmex account and wanted to start trading with leverage immediatly. As you can imagine, it was totally in the pants. And i went long (long means i bettet on an increasing Bitcoin price) on the Bitcoin / USD pair with a 50x leverage, and hell, this position rocked everything! I was 120% in profit and i thought i will be a millionaire the next day. As i saw about 1 BTC in my trading account i got incomprehensibly greedy. I was really convinced Bitcoin will make a new all time high and i will have a 1000% return on my trade. That's why i decided to let my position run and logged out of bitmex. I looked back in my account a few days later and saw my position continuing in big profit. So i turned my laptop off again and wanted to wait for the monster bullrun i expected. But what happened? One day Bitcoin dumpt so damn violently that i got liquidated immidiatly. I literally lost all of my funds on bitmex and stood in front a heap of rubble. I asked myself: How could this happen? Why did i just not close the position? Why the fuck am i such an shitty idiot? And the answer was clear: I really had not understood trading and proper risk management yet. Everyone who lost a huge amount of money knows this terrible feeling. The hopelessness, this incredible burning in your chest. Such an experience has a huge influence on a traders psychology. You just feel inferior and think you'll never get back up.

That's the point where you have to make a decision. Do you want to flicker and stop trading? Or do you want to pinch your ass and go get what you deserve? I decided on the second option. And i would recommend you to do the same! And if you want to have succes in trading this is the point you start *managing your risk* properly.

But what is adequate risk management about?

Plan your trades

It is about setting a predefined plan you act on. As the famous chinese militar general Sun Tzu's said: „Every battle is won befor it is fought." You can have a streak of luck, but you can also fail 10 trades in a row. That's not uncommon. Without managing your risk properly, this can be your game over. The most important goal is to keep the wheel turning and to stay in the game. I want to give you a short example. If you loose 10% of your money, you have to gain 11.1% to be break even again. If you are loosing 50% of your net worth, you have to double your money to make up the loss. The higher the loss, the more you have to recover. The key rule for new traders is to never risk more than maximum 2% of your money on a trade. (personally i would recommend to risk max. 1-1.5%).Only risk 2% of my money? But i only got 1000$, does this mean i should start trading with 20$, sir? Of course not.

If you want to enter a trade with your 1000$, you have to make some calculations first: entry price, stop loss, risk size and a take profit.

As the *risk size* is clear at 1-2%, you are searching your *entry price*. That's were the indicators and analyse techniques we learned come in to play. So you found a point you would enter the trade after you looked at the indicators.

Now you are searching for the *stop loss*. Usually it's like the other side of a broken trendline or under a support if we break trough. As we know the essentials of technical analysis we will find our stop losses. It's essential that you decide a stop loss *before* you enter a trade. And you will *not* widen your stop loss after you made your decision. You can move it to or above your entry price to secure your wins, but extending it downwards is absolutly *forbidden.*

Now we have to calculate how much money we are allowed to invest in our trade and I would highly recommend you to do this, because if you size your positions to big you will be massivly emotional attached to the trades your making, what often leads to false decisions and huge losses.

*Position size = (risk * budget) / entry price – stop loss price)*

This formula is universal and can be applied to every financial market.

So let's have an example: You want to trade with your 1000$ and found an altcoin currently trading at 4$ per unit. Your stop loss is 3$. So we are calculating: (1% * 1000$) / (4$ - 3$) = 10 / 1 = 10, so you are allowed to buy 10 coins for this trade.

An other example: risk size, budget and entry are clear, but we are setting our stop loss much tighter. Risk=1%, budget=1000$, entry=4$, stop loss=3.80$

(1% * 1000$) / (4$ - 3.80$) = 10$ / 0.20$) = 50, so you are allowed to buy 50 coins with this settings

We notice, the tighter the stop loss, the bigger the position size.

Now we will see a very interessting example. If we increase our risk a little bit and tighten our stop loss even more, we see a confusing position size:

Risk=1.5%, budget=1000$ entry=4$, stop loss=3.95$

(1.5% * 1000$ / (4$ - 3.95$) = 15$ / 0.05$ = 300

Huh, but sir, i only have money to purchase 200 coins?

Yes, and that's the point margin trading come into play. If you have calculated your position size properly, you are able to extend your position size and trade with a *leverage*. Because this sort of trading involves a very high risk, i would recommend you to do it only if you are experienced in normal trading. We will come back to leverage trading in the next chapter.

Another key rule to succes in trading is: never chase a pump or dump and do not overtrade. For example, once i got liquididated because i countertraded a big bitcoin dump with high leverage, i saw bitcoin dumped to much for the small volume and expected a corrective move upwards soon. That's why i choosed a high leverage, i think the position size was about 150.000$ As i a) didn't calculated the position size and b) did not set the stop loss correctly, bitcoin dumped even more and my stop loss wasnt triggered because of to fast falling prices. At the end of the day i lost a few thousand bucks and was sad as fuck. Don't do this! If you see big, irrational movements in the market, always wait for the market to calm down and to consolidate. Also, if you make a fault in this size, don't trade riskier just to make up your losses. This will break your neck, believe me. To overtrade is one of the biggest mistakes you can make. You as a trader has to act like a sniper. Fast, aggresive, but everytime on point. To shoot around won't kill your enemie, but one simple, clear shot will.

But is there any step for step tutorial how to start and catch a trade?

Luckily yes, the following page should be your protocol to plan a trade.

First of all you should plan every trade you make. Under which circumstances will i enter the trade? When do i close the position? What has to happen that my setup is invalid?

1. Look at the chart in the timeframe you prefer. As we learnd previously, our indicators and patterns are working in multiple timeframes.

2. After you found a good trade ask yourself: Is the price at a suppport / resistance level? Are the indicators matching to my plan? If you can answer this questions with yes, go ahead, if not, don't trade!

3. If i enter the trade, under which circmunstances will i buy and sell?

4. Where will be my stoploss? Under which circumstances will i leave the trade earlier? When is my setup invalid?

5. Position size = (risk * budget) / entry price – stop loss price

6. Setting a limit order to purchase the asset at the best price.

7. Do not make yourself crazy about your trade. If you calculated a proper position size you should have a really good chill.

8. Give your trade some time to perform.

9. Check if the trade is still matching to your trading plan. If yes let it play out, if not, try to leave the position with a minimum loss.

If you act after this short instructions, you have very good chances to be profitable even if you don't have a clue of indicators and markets.

Risk-reward ratio:

Another thumb rule to trade succesfully is to calculate the risk-reward ratio to your trades. This means: How many money i'm ready to loose in comparison to the possible gains?

I would recommend you to only take a trade with a R/R of 2. This means: If your entry is 10$, your planned exit is at 12$ and your stop loss is at 9$, your R/R is 2:1. You risk 1$ to gain 2$. A worse risk-reward ratio is no acceptable trade! Of course it is always better to have a higher R, for example forw every dollar you risk, 3 dollars oder 5 to gain.

Order types

As knowledge about trading is useless, if you don't know how to buy and sell an asset, we are now looking at the different order types you should be aware off. An order is a set buy or sell signal which will be executed once your preset parameters are hit.

So how to make a simple markets buy?

<u>The Limit buy order</u>

A limit order is the easiest way to purchase a crypto currency. In this example we saw Ethereum in our buy zone and wanted to purchase 5 units with the limit order (Default) type.

Quantity

The quantitiy describes how much units we want to purchase. If you enter a number here, Bittrex will calculate the estimated Bitcoin value of your order automatically.

Bid price

The bid price is the price per unit you want to purchase. You can enter your wanted value, but you can also chose between the current bid, ask and the last price. The last price describes the price in which the last trade occurs. It could be described as the fairest price between bid and ask.

Total

This is the absolute price of Bitcoin you have to afford for 5 Ethereum. In this example about 0.35BTC

The limit sell order

The limit sell order is the equivalent to the limit buy order.

Now we want to sell our Ethereum for profit, we bought at 0.07BTC per unit, now we are selling for 0,075BTC per unit. Great deal! But remember: This is no stop loss! If you are setting this order thinking of a stop loss you will get kicked out of your posititition on market price and may have to realise losses!

Now the most important order: The stop loss

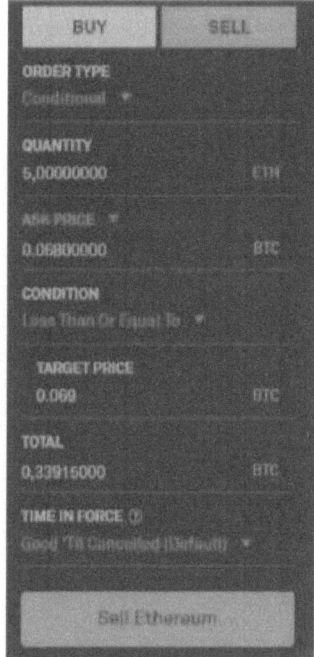

The stop loss order

As we learned before, managing our risk is one of the key ingredients of succesful trading. That's why we are looking at the conditional stop loss now.

First we are changing the order type from limit(default) to *conditional*.

Than we are entering our quantitiy like at a normal sell.

The ask price

The ask price is like a normal sell order. It describes the price, at we are willed to sell our Ethereum. In this case at 0,068BTC per ETH.

Condition

The condition is the decisive point for the stop loss. For a stop loss we are choosing the less than or equal to condition. This means, if the price is less than or equal to our chosen target price below, we will sell our coins at the ask price.

→ if the price falls to 0.069BTC or lower per ETH, our sell order will come in the market at 0.068BTC per ETH.

We can also set a conditional order as a buy, the advantage of this is that we can locate buy zones at don't have to wait for the price coming into it. We can set the order and if the prices falls below a certain level, the order will be added to the order book and is getting executed automatically.

As we can see here, if the price is less than or equal to 0.069, we will buy ETH at 0.0695 per   Unit.

40

As we now know how to spot a trade, how to manage risk and how to set an order – we are ready for the advanced fun.

Trading leveraged futures

The royal discipline in trading are futures with a leverage. But what is a future?

Futures

A future is a form of the derivate trading. Simply explained future contracts are a instrument that allows you to speculate on the future price of an asset, until the contract expires at the expiring date. Futures are a part of derivates, which also contain CFDs, Options and many more financial instruments.

Futures are much riskier than normal trading because of the probably high *leverage*. For example if you own 1 Bitcoin, you can „lend" money from your broker and trade with 10, 50 or even 100BTC. As you can imagine, you can make unbelievable high returns on your invest, but you can also loose way more than in trading without leverages.

For example: 1BTC=10000$, you go long, bitcoin goes up to 10500$

10x leverage → 50% gain (5000$)

50x leverage → 250% gain (25000$)

100x leverage → 500% gain (50000$)

But as you can imagine, if Bitcoin goes down 500$ and you didn't set a stop loss, you are totally fucked up. Happily you can't go into debt on cryptoexchanges so that your position would just be liquidadet at the liquidation price and you would loose all of your funds set in the trade. In this case you would loose 1 BTC.

But where to trade Bitcoin futures?

I would recommend you to trade on BitMEX.com, as i think it's simple to understand and the most reliable exchange at the moment. You can trade BTC/USD and many Altcoin/Bitcoin pairs there.

Long

„I'm long on Bitcoin – ATH soon!" - A sentence you probably heard a few times. But whats long? Long or Call means that you are speculating on increasing prices of the asset you are trading.

Short

Short or Put is the exact opposite, you are speculating on falling prices.

As we could see in the last months, trading on BitMEX is getting more and more popular. But i would recommend you to really take care. There are many Telegram groups or private discords outthere taking your money to give you „special calls" for stellar gains. You can purchase abonnements for about 0.1 BTC for 3 Months etc. This is total crap! You can find many good groups educating and giving trading signals for free. On the other hand, you should be able to analyse the market as good as them, and if you adapt to a proper risk management you will be able to trade on BitMEX totally profitable too. You should always be confident with your own analysis. If you are buying after some Twittertraders calls, you have to ask yourself first: Could this be a good trade? Are the parameters matching my preset trading plan? If not, why is the person on twitter or telegram shilling it? Does the person maybe have a personal interest to make up her or his own losses and is dumping on you? What i want to convince you of, is that you *always* do your own research on a trade you are going to make. It's your hard earned money, and the twitter trader who sits on the other half of the earth won't care about your loss if he sells in profit. I don't want to say that twitter traders are scammers, their are many really reliable, authentic caracters around – but you should be aware of them who aren't.

A highly profitable strategy whilst trading with leverage is called *scalping*. And no, i'm not talking about Inglorious Bastards and catching Nazi scalps, but the theory is maybe a bit correlating. Scalping means to enter a trade for a very short period of time. For example the retrace after touching a resistance or to go long if a support is touched. In this cases, the market is recovering for short periods of time very often. For example: We saw a former support on Bitcoin at 6800$ turning to a resistance. The resistance gained strength because price pulled back two times when touching it. So we see a possibility to scalp a few dollars out of the market. That's why we are setting a *limit selling order* on about 6800$. If we trade with 1 BTC and using a 10x leverage, we have a total amount of about 68000$ in our position. The essence of scalping is then waiting for a few dollards retrace. Let's assume the price went back up to 6814, we started our short at 6800, then price starts falling again. After we learned how to manage a stop loss, we are setting it break even and moving it further in our direction. After the price reaches to maybe 6770 or our predefined take profit zone, we close our positoin within about a few minutes to maybe an half hour. We made 30$ on our trade, leveraged with 10 → 300$ quick profit. There are many traders doing this the whole day, if you have time and muse, you can make huge gains everyday. But this style of trading can easily lead to stress and overtrading, that's why i would recommend you to start it slowly. I remember a trader, his name is @philakonecrypto, he has livestreams sometimes -and shit- this guy is killing it. I saw many position traders making fun of him, but i really have to say this guys trading is insane. He spots endless oppurtunities for scalps and is making big money on it everyday whilst playing videogames. Haha!

An other trading strategy is the *swing trading*. So you are holding your position several days to a few weeks. I would say this is the most common and the easiest way to start trading futures. You have enough time for your analysis and you aren't in a hurry to jump into rash positions. That's why it isn't that bad when your position tends in a loss a bit on the beginning as your trade has enough time to evolve well. But how to trade swings? In a trend market are a good opportunities to catch great swingtrades. In a bulltrend for example, you see a increasing price, than a correction, than a increasing price again. And as *the trend is your friend*, your searching for a possible LONG entry. But how could that work? As in normal tutorials you will get fined examples, i choosed a classical uptrend which isn't that simple as it may looks like in other trading tutorials. You can see the

ETH/USDT chart here, we see a strong up movement and a retrace to the trendline several times.

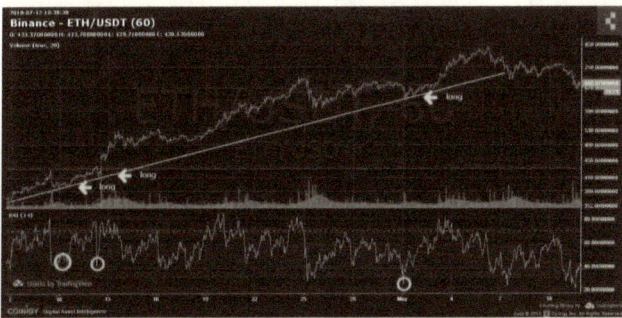

The RSI shows as a good buy opportunity + the price is touching the trendline several times. If you don't have a very good feeling for the markets i would be cautios to enter a position in not clear defined areas. You can also short the retracements to the trend line, but this is way riskier in a bull market as you can see in the chart above. You can do this in different timeframes as the theory works in every frame. But remember: The bigger picture is way more meaningful than the short term impression.

We apply the exact opposite theory on a bear market. What does this mean? We short from the trendline resistances. As you can see this method ages very well, that's why we remember: The trend is your friend. It's highly uncommon and very difficult to spot the exact reversal, in the most cases trying to catch a falling knife will run your trade into your stop loss. That's not what we want.

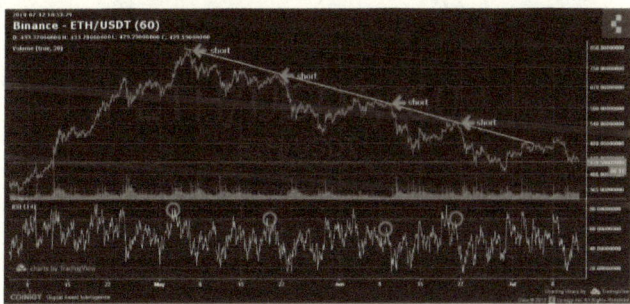

Countertrading trends are often no good idea. In the most cases you won't spot the reversal and you are going to loose money.

But how to trade a sideways market, which we are seeing way more often in the cryptospace today? We are using horizanl supports and resistances and try to catch trades between this areas. First we are drawing horizontal lines at every support and resistance zone notable. As a sideways market with no clear direction is way more difficult to trade, many traders are scalping at this point.

I will show you a chart, where you can see that we see massiv bullish divergences which could lead us to many false trades. That's why we have to be very patient during this markets. In this case our volume analysis should also come deeper into play because we can't be sure if the price acts after our indicators. A simple rule is: If the market comes to a resistance an we don't have a high buying volume, *short* the market. If it comes to a support which is about to break without high sell volume, *long* the market. If you can spot bullish RSI divergences, long the market after the second higher low of the RSI.

As you can see, we have several bullish divergences which would lead us to false trades if we would just long the RSI lows signal. That's why i would recommend you to really stay relaxed when trading futures.

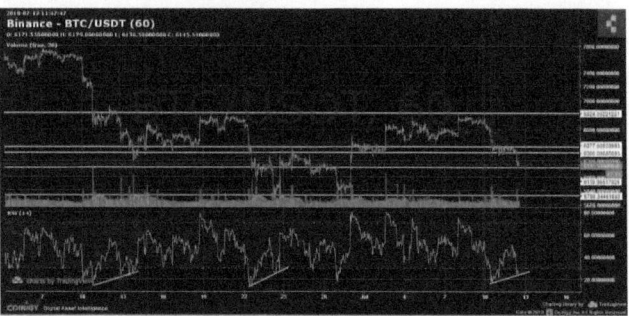

As we saw this pattern two times already, we are speculating that a similar case could occur. So we would go long on this indication. And we are rewarded.

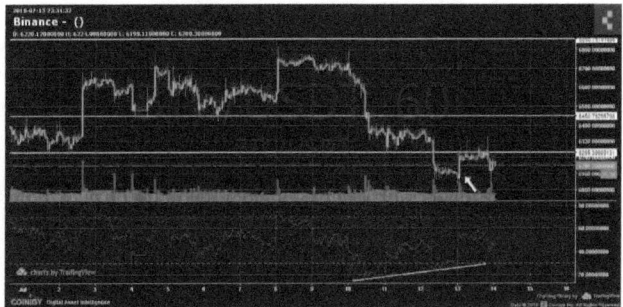

So we see once again, divergences are a strong sign for upcoming pumps and dumps. We will investigate this circumstance in the next chapter even further on bigger timeframes.

As you now have some ideas how to handle the futures market, you will be prepared to make your first own experiences.

Advanced (Charting/Investing - „Hodling")

After we learned many things about trading and technical analysis in general, we are heading towards to a more crypto related art of investing. The maxime „hodl till moon" is omnipresent like a mantra in the cryptospace. The important thing many people forget is, that what comes up, have to come down too. In the cryptospace this cirmcumstance is to observe especially at like every altcoin trades against btc. That's as safe as the amen in a curch. Sometimes you can't even make a cup of tea without loosing 30% of your portfolio value because of a major dump on altcoins after they rallyed. That's why you definitely should follow some rules trading altcoins.

First of all you should know, that markets are moving in cycles. Every market follows a cycle, some faster, some slower. As the crypto market is a very new, inefficient market it is moving way faster than a traditional market. That's also the cause that you have to chance to create incredible returns on your investmens in very short periods of time.

The most common terms to describe a cycle are: expansion, boom, recession and depression. Many of you have learned this in school years back and thought y tho i never gonna need this shit again. That's the point your former teacher would laugh at you. Fuck yes we need something from school now! So ask yourself, when is the perfect time to buy an asset? At the boom? At the recession? Yes, many uneducated investors would think so. And that's the point why many retail investors are getting wrecked so bad in the crypto market. Most people starting investing when a price is already increasing and the asset is on every newspaper, in the late night news and everybody is talking about. But that's exact the opposite time to invest. It's so incredible dumb. But yes, it is really logical why people are doing this failure. We see that an asset is growing in value, so we think it is well priced and furthermore a good investment. But you have to realize, that this is the point were the big business is over for the longest time. The early investors are taking profits now as everybody knows about the seemingly good invest. That is also the point were most retail investors will never get above. They don't realize that the markets pricing is the worst in periods of big booms. And it is totally obvious, that it's against the human nature and our deepest emotions to buy an asset which is literally on the ground not moving. But this is the zone for maximum financial opportunitie.

It is as simple as this. You have to buy when the streets are full of blood. And sell when everybody is talking about investing.

It's no joke, during the last crypto run in decembre 2017 my girlfriend went to work with the train, and an old lady over 70 years started asking her about crypto. If she knows things about, what is the next bitcoin and that she had invested a huge amount of their life savings to buy a few Bitcoins. I have to think of this lady from time to time, because i think this is the perfect example for a bubble popping. If she holds till now, she probably has lost about 70% of her investment. That's really shitty, for real. And as we don't want this to happen to us or our friends and family members, we are trying to get over the human emotions and trying to start investing *rational*. Another tip i want to give you on your way: There are people everywhere saying: „This time it's different". Believe me, it is not. The market will crash because the market is born to crash. It is undoubtly in the DNA of the market to go trough phases of recession and depression. Everyone who talks of the opposite is simply wrong. A good example is the investment strategy of Charly Munger and Warren Buffet. They are sitting on cash at least for near a decade waiting for the market to crash. And i think, nobody can argue against the success of Berkshire Hathaway.

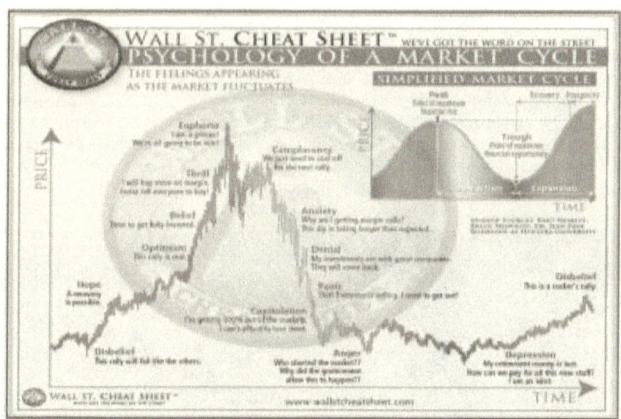

So, back to business. How to handle and how to spot market cycles? On cryptotwitter we see one special picture over and over again. I think the problem is, it is really good to understand so i want to show it to you: The wallstreet cheat sheet.

This picture describes the altcoin market so exact. You could overlap every altcoin chart and will see the similarities. And if you don't want to monitor the market at least a few times a week to do your trades, this could be the better opportunitie for you. But the problem is, the way down after a rallye is much longer than the way up, and the way down hurts twice after not selling the top. That's why you should be clear minded and have a good plan. And i am sure, you will really appreciate it when you act accordingly to your plan.

So let's have a deeper look at the altcoin market cycles. When do altcoins pump?

When we compare Bitcoin with altcoins, we can easily see that they are correlating in a high manner. But: If the Bitcoin dominance is higher than 45%, altcoins tend to dump whilst bitcoin rallyes. This means: When Bitcoin goes up, altcoins tend to go up to. This is not a all in one solution because many other factors are playing in too. (Fundamental news, hacks, etc.) But on the whole this is a good approach to understand the behaviour of the crypto markets. This phenomen is caused by the tradig pairs. You need to buy Bitcoin, to purchase an altcoin. Also you need to sell your altcoin into bitcoin to cash out dollars. I think it is quit possible that the BTC/altcoin pairs will undock in the future, because many exchanges are releasing USD trading pairs. But the correlation will last for a while i think. As Bitcoin is the flagship of the cryptospace and also one of the safest currencys, people tend to evaluate the whole market in relation to bitcoins performance. That means, if bitcoin isn't performing good, people will rather go into fiat instead of going into altcoins. But as we learned previously, when assets are in depression stage, we as investors have the highest financial opportunity. That's why the market cycle trader pays attention at exact this patterns. But what does a bottom look like? A bottom is marked by a few good visible signs. The simplest way to spot a bottom is to zoom out. Switch at least to the 1D timeframe and zoom out as wide as you can. You will see areas where the price is totally high and areas in which the price is falling back and bobs up and down for a while. This price area is called the *accumulation area*. When we are looking for longer invests, we <u>only</u> buy in this areas. An other great sign to spot a bottom is the volume. If the price isn't moving for weeks or months occupied with very low volume we start paying attention. But how does a accumulation zone look like?

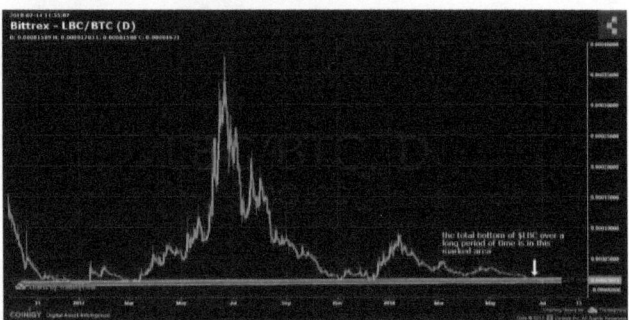

A perfect example i want to give you is the chart of $LBC. Library Credits is like a dezentralized youtube. So let's have a look:

You see the bottom zone? The price was their a few times, not moving much and started to grow again.

Another example $COVAL.

48

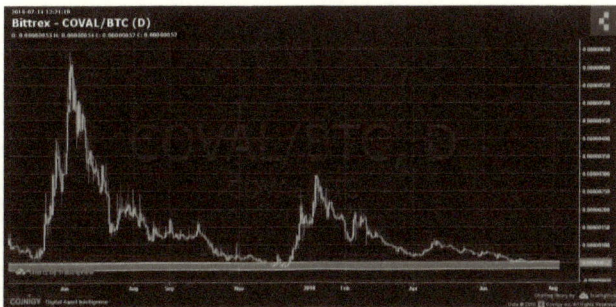

If you are clicking trough altcoin charts on bigger timeframes you will recognize this pattern over and over again.

A good strategy to accumulate altcoin on their bottom is to set staggered buy orders. So let's assume you want to invest 0.1BTC in an altcoin of your choice. You think your altcoin has hit the bottom and should start growing anytime soon. First of all you spot the accumulation area. This means in which price zone is the asset moving during the accumulation? If the altcoin is moving between 1000-1500 satoshis you are splitting your amount of Bitcoin at leat in 3 parts. So you set your first buy order with 0.033BTC value on 1400 sats to have a safe buy. Then you set your second buy order way lower at maybe 1100 sats. The third part of your bitcoins you keep in the background observing what the price is doing. Is the price falling trough the 1000 sats? A even better buy to averaging down your accumulation. Is the price breaking out of accumulation range? If you are sure the price is going to moon, then buy at a bit higher price. If not, hold it in the background again and try to spot an other good buying opportunitie.

If you are searching for hidden gems on smaller exchanges like cryptopia, you can observe a very low daily volume. Take care in this case, building a position in a illiquid market is way more tricky than in a liquid market. If you purchase 0.2BTC of an altcoin, but the daily volume is only 0.1BTC you are able to pump the price out of accumulation range which can lead to a market reversal on this trading pair. But as you want an entry as cheap as possible you should set very low buy orders with little amounts of $BTC.

So you bought a bunch of your favorite altcoins on the accumulation zone and it starts pumping. But hey? Where do i take profits ?

There are a few ways to take profit. The safest and most reliable is to also set staggered sell orders accordingly to the growth of the asset. This means that you try to spot *major resistances* and sell into them. So we are analyzing our former high and setting some orders. In our $LBC example this could look like this:

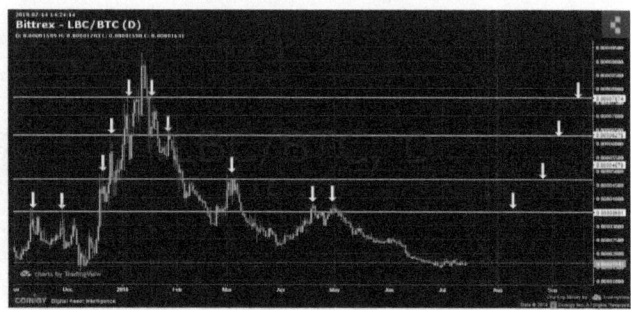

After you spotted the possible sell zones, you should take at least the RSI indicator to help. You can easily identify divergences which really often lead to a *major reversal* on the daily timeframe. If you are a risk taker, you could base your whole buying and selling strategy on spotting divergences in a big timeframe. If you can spot big bearish divergences, it's really time to exit the market. But riding this divergences can create a massiv higher return of invest than just spotting prices to sell. In many cases the market is getting unbelievable irrational when altcoins spiking up a few 100% in less than a month. That's why even if the demand is signifcantly decreasing, the people keep pushing the price to new highs. But you should be totally sceptical if you see such a divergence. I will show you a few examples where bearish divergences leaded to a massive drop in price, and you will recognize that they are literally everywhere.

First the last Bitcoin bubble in decembre 2017:

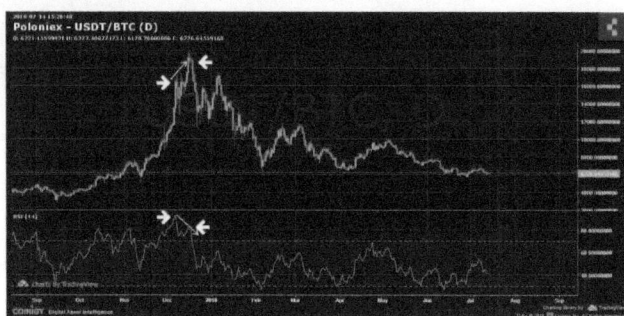

Second literally every altcoinchart you can look at.

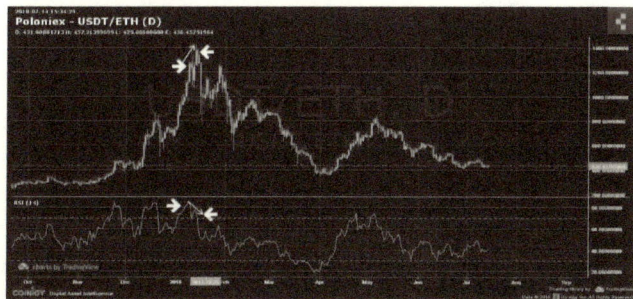

ETH/USD:

You can see this pattern over and over again. This is why a bearish divergence is so powerful. You see, you could overlay any of this charts with the wall street cheat sheets describing of a markets cycle. That's also why we know that we are coming in accumulation zone again. You can also spot this bearish divergence pattern on May 2018 if you take a deeper look at the chart. And this leads us to another major lesson. How can we evaluate how long the market is still rising? How can we spot the overall trend to optimize our exits?

Luckily we can get a view of the current market situation. As we know markets are moving in waves and cycles, we can pretty good evaluate in which state the market is. We can use the market buy percentage indicator for example. The market buy percentage is a free tool from turtlebtc.com. It could be described as an RSI indicator applied on the whole market. So we can spot trends, their end and possible reversals. So let's have a look on this indicator:

As you can see, when writing this it's the 16th of july 2018. We see the whole market was massivly oversold the last weeks and months and starts recovering now. This is a sign for us that we hit the bottom and shoud build our long term positions soon to get the best entrys. So, if our indicators, the chart analysis and the buy market percentage signaling us

51

that we are at the bottom, we have the biggesst financial opportunity. And we are well prepared to use it!

On the other hand, the buy market percentage indicator warns us of potential upcoming reversals and helps us to spot vergy good exits combined with our other indication.

So, to get a clearer picture of how we could apply the buy market percentage indicator on the whole crypto ecosystem, we start to compare the signals of it with the global market capitalization.

We will start with the decembre run in 2017. We see that Bitcoin peaked at 17th decembre at 19.800$ with a massiv bearish RSI divergence which was the first indicator for an reversal. After Bitcoins peak, the mass of new investors discovered exchanges and altcoins and pumped up the market excluding bitcoin in a unbelievable manner. Coinmarketcap shows us that we peaked was at 7th january 2018 with an global market capitalization of around 830 Billion dollar. The Bitcoin price at this date was around 17.000$. So in average, the 7th january of 2018 were the perfect date to exit all positions and enjoying the profits of this huge run.

The buy market percentage indicator peaked at the 27th decembre, loosing steem till the 7th. Now take care: While the buy market percentage indicator were decreasing, the prices increased further. What do we see? Also applied on the whole market we see *massiv divergences in comparing buy market percentage and global market capitalization*.

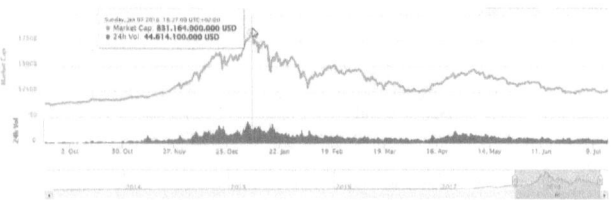

Here the coinmarketcap peak.

And the divergencing buy market percentage indicator on the 7th january.

52

Now we are comparing the last little run in april-may 2018.

Bitcoin was heading to 10.000$, alts were spiking up a few hundred percent. Many people were calling out for the „next altcoin bullrun". But what do we see analyzing our indicators?

Bitcoin peaked at the 5th may on around 10020$ with a massive RSI divergence. This time there weren't that much new investors around pumping coins. So the global market capitalization peaked at around 470 billion $ at the 5th may too. The buy market percentage indicator were declining rapidly whilst the prices were increasing further.

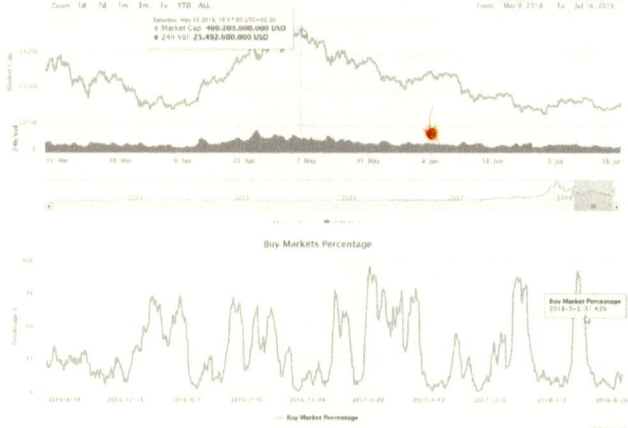

As you can see, the buy markets were decreasing very fast whilst the price climbed further up. The massive bearish divergence in Bitcoin, the divergence between the buy markets percentage and the global market capitalization were a very clear sign for a reversal.

What do we remember: We can spot reversals very precisely if we have a closer look to bearish divergences on the whole market. With this strategy you will be able to tracert the whole markets movement and evaluate what could occur next. Of course these predictions aren't 100% adaquat, but very very close.

So if we ask ourself when to finally get out of our positions, this is a major indication to know.

Even if i'm mostly a technical trader, i want to explain the fundamental analysis to you as well. In the cryptospace it's not easy to evaluate the fundamentals as we don't have a classical cashflow or a course book value ratio, that's why this chapter will be a little smaller.

Fundamental Analysis

Fundamental analysis on an invest is a very important factor to evaluate if an investmens could be gaining strength or not. As informations aren't that good verifiable in the crypto space and many false information are coming around, it's really difficult to evaluate the real fundamental value of an crypto asset. So we are working with the things we got to make our analysis as good as possible.

So let's pretend you found a project you could imagine to buy in. Ask yourelf:

How active is the development?

Normally you can trace every development step on the Github.com thread of the project. Every feature implemented and every step they took will be visible there.

Activity of the developers and the community

Check their telegram, twitter, discord channel – ask questions. Look if they are activly writing and informing over their progress. If not, the project could be dead already. Look at the Twitter channels of the developers, are they posting new stuff?

Are they only shitposting?

How are they acting in public?

Is the community big? Are they active believers or just rekt bagholders?

Try to understand the sentiment of their whole community, is it bad or good?

Are the developers delivering the releases accordingly to the roadmap in time?

What is the coin about? Is it a Bitcoin or Litecoin fork? If yes, why should it gain any value if it's just Bitcoin with other parameters?

Projects like Ethereum were that succesfull because they added value to the ecosystem. No, they are the ecosystem. They build the whole frame for the current development.

Is the project you are researching also adding value? If not, why should it grow?

Is there a project comparable to it? If yes, how big is it? If there are competeting projects this isn't bad at all, it could just give you an insight over the potential room to grow.

Is there a benefit for using a blockchain on this project? Or would it be cheaper, faster and easier to set up a zentralized system for this purpose?

If you assume that 99% of the crypto currencys fail, do you think this one will outlive the purge? If not, do you think there is short term growing potential because of good marketing, or reaching milestones on their roadmap etc.?

If you can answer the majority of this questions in a positive manner, the project you are looking for shouldn't be that bad!

Evaluating the development team

After you had a closer look in the social media performance of the project you are looking for, let's have a look at the development team in a whole. Normally they should be listed with their real names, pictures and their vita on the website. Usually there are also linked.in profiles connected to it. Research every single person, look if they achieved what they are telling. If not, don't invest! There are also plenty of scams out there, using very aggressive marketing and promising to be the next bitcoin. Don't trust them!

Did they had former companies or apps? What's with them? Are they trying to bring a gamechanger on the markets or are they just fishing money from the blockchain hype?

If the development team are who they are pretending, it's a really good sign.

Market capitalization

As mentioned earlier, the market cap of an project is totally important to determine the potential growth. In 2017 everybody screemed: „XVG next Bitcoin going to 10$!!" and many new investors followed this dump shills buying into XVG. The price spiked up about x30 and many sold with huge wins. But the problem of the new investors were, they didn't knew how the crypto markets work and they really believed XVG could hit 10$ soon. But if they would had a simple look at the circulating supply of XVG which is around 15.000.000.000 coins, they had to reach a market capitalization of 150.000.000.000$. This is more than 60% of the whole crypto capitalization at the moment writing this. So if they did this simple calculation, they would have realized that this price is totally unrealistic and simple never going to happen.

So as we learned earlier at the ICO chapter, calculate the market capitalization and be sceptical at projects with unbelievable high supply. (i.e 50000000000)

Spotting scams

If you are around on social media or just reading the newspaper, you will most likely come across people telling you they invented or working for a new crypto coin which will easily do an x100. In many cases it's a fromer friend which turned to a suitwearing „online marketing specialist" posing with a BMW and making holidays in Dubai. The same guy is promoting his forex trading whatsapp group in which he gives you 100% free, profitable trading signals. You know exactly which kind of person i mean, aren't you?

So they are giving seminars over „the blockchain revolution" and their new coin and why it will make everybody rich. (exept of you lol). We saw this so many times, everyhting started with OneCoin i guess, than Bitconnect, Platincoin, Homeblockcoin, blablabla. The thing i want to commit you. If someone is trying to sell you a coin, based on a multi level marketing structure, it is simply a ponzi scheme. Nothing more. You will invest money and you will loose it in 99% of the cases. Of course there are networkers with great downlines which are making a really good buck on this sort of projects, but after talking to them i know that even they are convinced of that they are selling nothing more than ponzi schemes. They just want the quick dollar. Free according to the motto: The last bites the dogs. This behaviour is afwul and this sort of people are cancer spreading and stealing the money of old innocent people which don't have a clue what they are investing in. So, but how to spot a scam in less than 5 Minutes?

1). Look if they have a multi level marketing structure

So, if they are offering a payment over several levels if you bring people to join their systems they are usually ponzi scams. Often they are split the profits like that:

1 level: 8% of the new members invest

2 level: 6% of the new members invest

3 level: 4% of the new members invest and so on.

Normally you have to reinvest your money or have to buy special packages to unlock the further levels which can bring you more money in the pyramide. That's how they are trying to keep the weel turning. The bad thing is only: One time no new investors will join the party and the whole organism collapses. In many cases the founders are millionaires by than anyway, but you lost your money. So take care!

2). Look at their whitepaper

In many cases the whitepaper of such a scam coin is not longer than 5 sites, describing a bit of the technology and then proclaming why they are the new Bitcoin and the invest of the century. The best thing i have ever seen was even a 100% accurate price calculation(LOL). They proclamed that the price will rise von 0.10 first to two, than to 5 dollars with dates preset! This shit is so unbelivable scammy. You simply cannot define the price of an asset previously because it is the middle between supply and demand in a healthy trading ecosystem. If anybody tells the price will reach 5$ because of a preset plan they have they are a) liars or b) cutting supply and pushing the price by manipulation theirselfs.

3). Are there publicly known networkers in the marketing?

Another good indicator for revealing a scam is looking for the people which are making the marketing. Are they any instagram life coachs posing in a CLA mercedes selling their „10 steps to succes" lifeplan or someting like that? If yes – run away!

But take care, there are also other multi level marketing scams outthere exept of coins. From time to time you will also see companies who are delivering for example cloud mining, or crypto trading with your capital based on an AI based algorithm concept. A good example is probably a company which was called „Cryp Trade Capital". The company said that they are employing high quality traders which are spotting the market 24/7 and trading with your capital! A bit like a investment fonds, but not serious and based on multi level marketing. Many people made a lot of money with it, but the most aren't even break even. One day the authorities took action and shuttet their service down as they hadn't licenes. And yes, the last bites the dogs. At this time i was working at a factory before starting to study, and i had a coworker. He and his friend took a credit over 50.000$ to invest in cryp trade capital. I didn't saw him again, but he has to be ultimately fucked up. I'm really sorry for him, this shit isn't cool.   What   i   am   trying   to   say: There   are so many scammers outthere trying to steal your money, please take care and don't believe anyone in this space! Not even me lol!

I think, you should be able to evaluate which projects are scam and which are probably a good investment. Now in the last chapter, i want to give you some trading ideas, setups ans simple technical analysis. I hope you can enjoy!

Chapter Five:

Charts and Trading Ideas

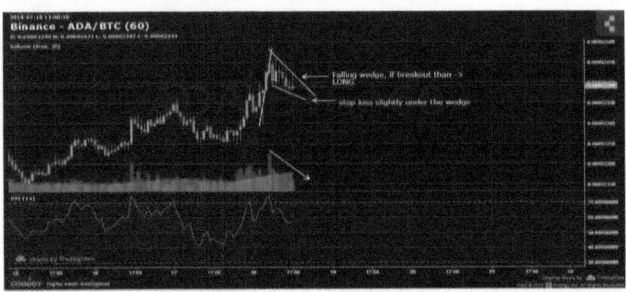

In this chapter i just want to give you some impressions on setups for a trade. Look closely and try to apply the previously learned stuff on this charts.

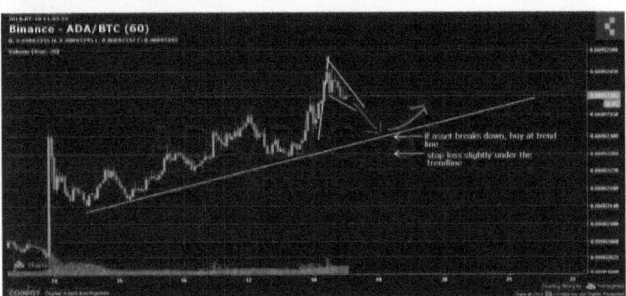

On the first picture you can see ADA in a falling wedge. As we learned it should breakout bullish. If it breaks out, we are waiting for the retest of the former resistance and starting to buy in. The stop loss should be slight under the flags support.

If the falling wedge breaks downwards, we see a strong trendline where we can catch the next possible trade. We are speculating that the trend will go on and start buying at the trendline support. Our stoploss is slightly under the trendline to avoid bigger losses if the trend   breaks.

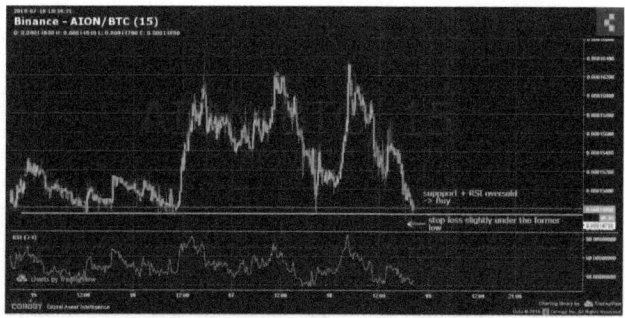

We see AION is going to hit the horizontal support. As the RSI is a bit oversold and the support seems to be strong, we see a opportunity to buy in. So we buy in the horizontal support and setting our stop loss slightly under the lowest low of the support.

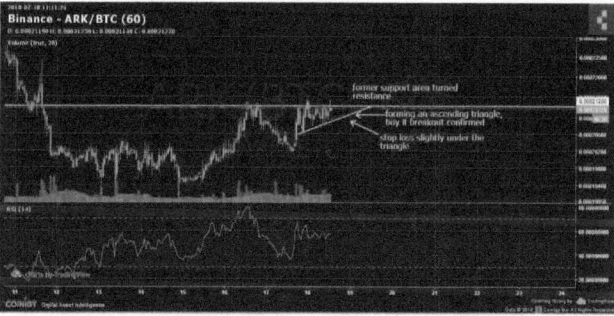

We can see an ascending triangle here on the ARK/BTC chart. We have a resistance area and an area which build higher lows. We expect that the price will break trough the resistance area. So we can have a good market buy here. The stop loss should be slight next to the triangles vertical support.

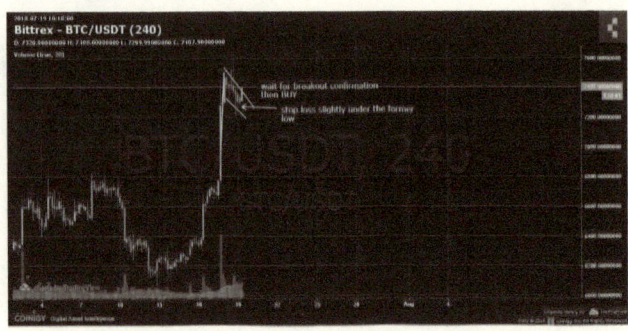

On this picture we see BTC/USD forming a bullflag on the 4H chart. We see a small breakout, but as the candle isn't finished yet we wait for confirmation to avoid a false breakout. If we know the breakout is approved, we buy in or go long with a leverage.

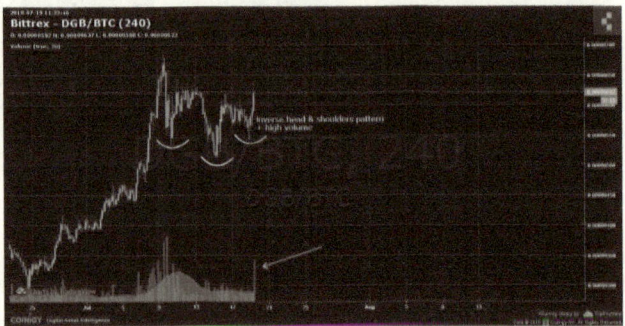

After a rallye on DGB, we see an inverse head and shoulders pattern is forming. The volume decreased from the left to the right shoulder, then the bulls took control and pushed the volume + price higher. Normally we see an head and shoulders pattern as a trend reversal. But in some special cases we can also spot them on trend continuations as a form of „consolidation".

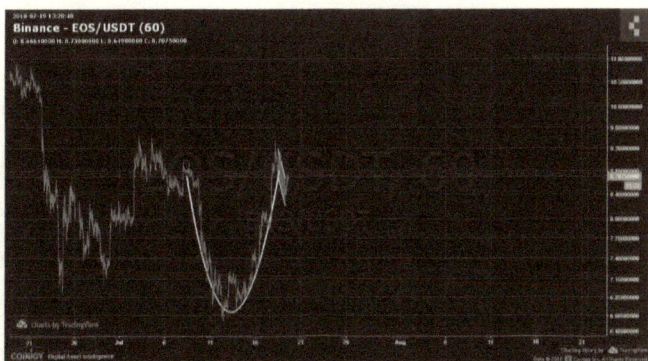

Here we can see a beautiful cup and handle pattern on the EOS/USDT chart. Normally we buy in here as a break out will occur in the most cases.

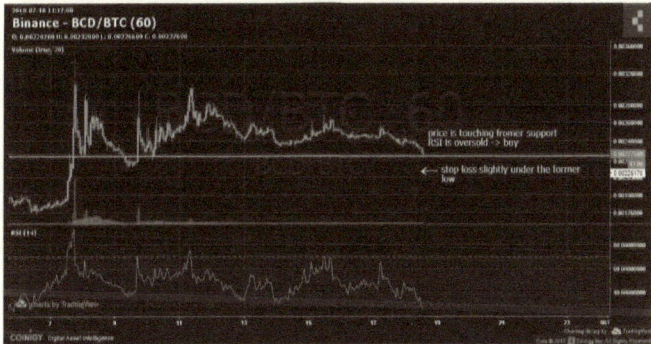

Here can we see a simple setup. BCD is coming to the support, the RSI is oversold so it signals us that this could be a good buy. As we can see that the asset formed a price slightly under the support once, we are setting our stop loss slightly under this low.

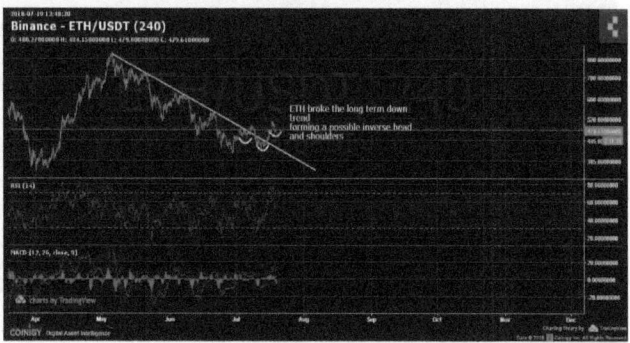

We can see here ETH broke the long term down trend against the USD and is probably forming an inverse head and shoulders pattern. As the RSI is a bit overbought i would wait for it to come down more and then set a good long term buy order at a good price level.

That's it. I hope you understood the dynamic of the crypto market at least a bit. If any questions are still open feel free to contact me:

Marius@altcoin.team

or hit me up on twitter @mariusBTC

Thanks for your audience!

Acknowledgements

First of all i want to thank you dear reader that you got till the end of this book. I really hope i was able to add value to your trading and i hope you will get succesful in this space. Further i want to thank all of my friends and believers, especially: Jonas R. (Blockchaincoach) for keep pushing me forwards and bringing me to the crypto space. Hell bro, you made it already! Now we have to make it too.

MrMax for the great design and layout of the book + the front and backcover

Louis W. for starting trading with me, our exchange of information and the great time we have!

I also want to thank my girlfriend carmen, she always believed in me which makes me the strongest man on the earth.

Of course i want to thank my mother and my dad, which are always kept believing that i will make something good. Also a big thank you to everyone helped me to correct this book, Jennifer A. Carmen M, Louis W, Max

I want to thank the Altcointeam as they are the engine of our group development and our staking pool solutions.

And at least i want to thank all the people saying: If it's that easy, everybody would do it. You are my motivation, and yes it's that easy – fuck you.

7

www.ingramcontent.com/pod-product-compliance
Lightning Source LLC
Chambersburg PA
CBHW020623220526
45463CB00006B/2658